THE ABORTION
DEBATE

Essential Viewpoints

THE ABORTION
DEBATE

BY COURTNEY FARRELL

Content Consultant
Ed Langerak, Professor of Philosophy
St. Olaf College

ABDO
Publishing Company

CREDITS

Published by ABDO Publishing Company, 8000 West 78th Street, Edina, Minnesota 55439. Copyright © 2008 by Abdo Consulting Group, Inc. International copyrights reserved in all countries. No part of this book may be reproduced in any form without written permission from the publisher. The Essential Library™ is a trademark and logo of ABDO Publishing Company.

Printed in the United States.

Editor: Nadia Higgins
Copy Editor: Paula Lewis
Interior Design and Production: Emily Love
Cover Design: Emily Love

Library of Congress Cataloging-in-Publication Data
Farrell, Courtney.
  The abortion debate / Courtney Farrell.
    p. cm. — (Essential viewpoints)
  Includes bibliographical references and index.
  ISBN 978-1-60453-053-7
  I. Abortion—United States. 2. Abortion—United States—History. 3. Abortion—Moral and ethical aspects. I. Title.

  HQ767.5.U5F37 2008
  363.460973—dc22

                        2007031913

TABLE OF CONTENTS

Activists on both sides of the abortion debate stage protests to voice their strong opinions.

A Sensitive Subject

When a woman gets an abortion, she is intentionally ending her pregnancy. Since abortion ends a developing human life, it is a sensitive subject. Some people are so opposed to abortion that they believe it should be illegal. Others believe a woman should have the right to make the choice of whether to have an abortion.

The question of abortion is a question about rights. Activists choose sides in the conflict depending on whose rights they most passionately defend. The fetus, the pregnant woman, her male partner, and the couple's parents all have advocates who defend their rights. In this debate, we see democracy in action.

Almost half of the pregnancies that occur in the United States are not planned. Approximately 40 percent of these pregnancies end in abortion. In other cases, mothers who may have been troubled by their pregnancies grow to love their babies. Still, 10 percent of newborn babies are reported as unwanted. Some situations are resolved by adoptive parents raising the baby. Other babies, often those of drug addicts or rape victims, are abandoned at hospitals. These babies receive care as wards of the state and eventually are put up for adoption. Children with physical and emotional disabilities are not likely to be adopted and are raised in orphanages.

Should abortion be a choice? Opinions differ, but one-third of U.S. women will have had an abortion by age 45.

PRO-LIFE VERSUS PRO-CHOICE

People who are opposed to abortion describe themselves as pro-life, while those who want abortion to remain legal consider themselves pro-choice. Pro-life activists suggest that women with unwanted pregnancies put their babies up for adoption instead of choosing abortion. Pro-choice groups counter that this option works for many women, but not for all.

Another group of people find themselves in the middle of the issue. While they would not say abortion is murder, they are uncomfortable with the destruction of a fetus. In their opinion, a fetus deserves special consideration because it has the potential to develop into a person. Many who hold this viewpoint are equally uncomfortable with legally forcing a woman to have a baby. To them, it is not the government's place to interfere with a woman's most intimate decisions. They worry that forcing a woman to have a baby could cause her serious harm—either physical, psychological, economic, or otherwise. People with this view often say they are "morally pro-life" but "legally pro-choice."

Whatever one's perspective on the ethics of abortion, individuals can better understand each other by considering the reasons a woman might make this choice.

ABORTION AND TEENAGERS

A pregnant teen may choose abortion for many reasons. Some girls may not want to tell their parents they are pregnant. Other girls want to prevent disruption to their lives or to avoid becoming the target of gossip.

Teenage girls who become pregnant must often choose between abortion and dropping out of school. Many schools do not

Two Women's Experiences with Abortion

The following stories are compilations of true personal accounts, and the names are not real.

- *Kelly's Story:*

"I was 17 when I had my abortion. I was afraid when I got pregnant; I didn't want to drop out of school and lose my chance at college. The abortion providers were kind, so things seemed ok at first. It wasn't until later that I began to really think about what I'd done. I've cried a lot since then, especially when I see babies or someone I know is happily expecting. I think about our baby, how old she would be, what she would have looked like. For some reason she's a girl in my mind; I never asked the doctor. It's been five years, but I think I'll never feel whole again."

- *Margot's Story:*

"I got pregnant during my second year of college. I wasn't serious about the guy, and he had no interest in marriage anyway. I went to the college clinic and got the abortion pill. It did make me sick for a couple of days. I went home and my roommates took care of me until the bleeding stopped. I could never have had a baby at that point in my life. The children I'll have someday will have an educated mom, with a good job. I wasn't going to let a pregnancy force me out of college and into some trailer park. Sure, I felt sad for a while, but I never regretted my decision."

allow pregnant girls to stay in school, although this policy has changed in some districts. Girls who leave school to raise a baby often live in poverty their entire lives. Also, children of very young mothers are more likely to develop emotional and cognitive (thinking and learning) problems. These problems are due more to effects of poverty than to the age of their mothers. Young mothers tend to be poor and may not be able to provide their children with a stimulating environment and quality child care.

Other Reasons for Abortion

Some families strongly discourage sex before marriage, so some women may want their sexual activity to remain a private matter. Girls who consider abortion may also be influenced by the negative attitudes about single mothers in their communities.

Other reasons for abortion include failure of contraception, especially in single or professional women who are not prepared to have a baby. Women who are mentally unstable, in abusive relationships, or addicted to drugs are also more likely to choose abortion. Survivors of rape or incest usually choose not to bear the child of their attacker.

Additionally, prenatal testing, or testing of the fetus, can reveal birth defects that would cause the baby to be disabled or even die. Even married couples who want children may choose to end such pregnancies.

There is a wide range of opinions on whether abortion is ethical, and if so, under what conditions. People who believe abortion is acceptable only in certain cases usually make their decisions based on the age of the fetus and the reason the woman is seeking the abortion.

The Heart of the Controversy: When Does Human Life Begin?

Pro-choice advocates believe that abortion is not murder because the fetus is not yet truly human, but pro-life advocates disagree. Disagreement exists within activist groups, too. Some people who are pro-choice oppose late-term abortions, and some people who

How Does a Woman Know She Is Pregnant?

Women who are not pregnant menstruate, or get their period, each month. Usually the first sign of pregnancy is a missed period, though some women feel morning sickness, or nausea and vomiting upon waking.

Some women do not realize they are pregnant right away. While women do not menstruate while they are pregnant, some bleeding—which looks like a period—may occur in the early months of pregnancy. Also, teenage girls often do not get their periods on a regular schedule. So it is more difficult for them to know if they have missed a period.

Pregnancy tests can be purchased at drug stores. These tests are accurate 97 percent or more of the time. More accurate tests can be obtained from a doctor or a pregnancy clinic.

Gestation Period	Appearance and Activity of Fetus
1 day	The embryo is a single cell.
First month	Smaller than a grain of rice, the embryo is not yet recognizable as a human. The heart is beating, and the nervous system has begun to form.
Third month	About as long as an adult's thumb, the fetus can be recognized as human, with completely formed feet and hands.
Fourth month	The mother can feel the fetus moving.
Fifth month	About one pound (.45 kg), the fetus takes on a "newborn" appearance.
Sixth month	Some babies born now will survive, although they risk disability and will require intensive care.
Seventh month	If born now, most infants will survive with special care. Weight is about three pounds (1.4 kg).
Eighth month	The baby is likely to survive independently if born now.
Ninth month	The baby is ready to be born.

The development of a fetus

are pro-life approve of abortion in cases of rape or incest.

The controversy centers on when the fetus becomes fully human. Does the fetus become a true human being, with full human rights, when the sperm fertilizes the egg? Or does it gradually become more human as it develops? If so, when? Does it become human at quickening, when the mother can feel the fetus moving? Or does it happen at viability, when the fetus is developed enough to survive outside the womb? Or does the fetus gain rights only at birth? It is very difficult for people to agree on the answers to these questions. People make their decisions based on their own religious and ethical viewpoints.

WHEN ABORTIONS ARE PERFORMED

The first trimester of pregnancy is from conception through 12 weeks. Approximately 88 percent of abortions occur in the first trimester, and almost 60 percent of these are performed before nine weeks of pregnancy. The second trimester extends from 12 weeks through the end of the twenty-seventh week. About 12 percent of abortions occur in the second trimester, and only 1.2 percent of abortions occur when the pregnancy is at 21 weeks or more. The third trimester is from 24 weeks through delivery. Only 0.01 percent of all abortions are performed at this stage of development. Such late-term abortions are performed only in extreme medical situations.

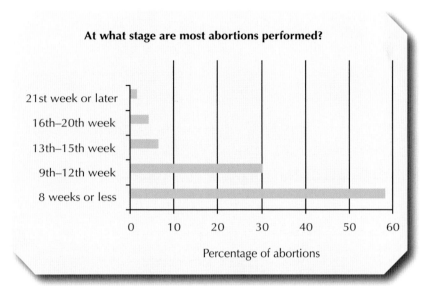

At what stage are most abortions performed?

21st week or later	
16th–20th week	
13th–15th week	
9th–12th week	
8 weeks or less	

Percentage of abortions

Two Types of Abortions

Abortions can be medical or surgical. Medical abortions use drugs to end a pregnancy, while surgical abortions physically remove the embryo or fetus from the uterus.

Medical abortions are effective only if the woman has been pregnant nine weeks or less. Either of two drugs is prescribed to end the pregnancy. Then another medication is taken a few days later to start contractions in the uterus (tightening of the muscles in the womb). This should empty the uterus. Women experience bleeding, pain, cramping, and sometimes fever during the process.

According to the National Abortion Federation (NAF), an organization of abortion providers, medical abortion is very safe. The group also says that a medical abortion will not hinder a woman's chances of getting pregnant again in the future.

Rarely, medical abortion does not work. Babies that survive medical abortions are at risk of being born deformed. That is why women undergoing medical abortions are instructed to return to the clinic for follow-up examinations and a surgical abortion if necessary.

The pro-life group National Right to Life Committee (NRLC) questions the claim that medical abortion is safe. The NRLC literature highlights a case in which an Iowa woman came close to death after losing at least half her blood. The NRLC also feels that there is not enough evidence to make a judgment about the long-term effects of medical abortions.

Surgical abortions are now performed with a method called vacuum aspiration. During this procedure, a woman is put under mild sedation or total anesthesia. Her cervix (opening to the uterus) is then opened and the contents of the uterus are suctioned out. The woman experiences mild to severe cramping and pain during and after the procedure.

Surgical abortions are usually performed during the first and second trimesters, and very rarely in the third trimester. Usually third-trimester abortions occur only if tests show that the fetus has severe defects, or if continuing the pregnancy would threaten the mother's life.

Complications from the surgery include infection or bleeding. Doctors also monitor for blood clots in the uterus and tearing of the cervix or uterus. According to the NAF, these complications usually occur in fewer than 1 percent of cases.

The American Life League publishes very different statistics on the aftermath of surgical abortion. The group says that 10 percent of women suffer immediate complications, one-fifth of which are life threatening. The group also believes the procedure could keep a woman from becoming pregnant again.

One thing both pro-life and pro-choice groups can agree on is that abortion risks do increase as a pregnancy progresses.

A teenage mother drops off her son at a day care program at her high school in Minneapolis, Minnesota.

A Puritan wedding in New England during the 1600s

ABORTIONS FROM PAST
TO PRESENT

1327 English law made abortion legal at any time during pregnancy. In England, abortion was still legal by 1670, but the American colonies had different rules. In the colonies, abortion was illegal, though it did not carry as severe a penalty as murder.

Colonial America, 1670–1807

Records from early America reveal a society quite different from the morally strict one often portrayed in stories. Although the colonies were founded by stern religious groups, sex before marriage was not uncommon. Records detailed marriages and births in the colonies. They also revealed that, before 1680, 3 percent of newly married women gave birth within six months of their marriage, and 8 percent had babies in fewer than nine months from their wedding day. This trend continued over time, and from 1760 to 1800, one-third of all brides gave birth to their first child in less than nine months of marriage. There was little dishonor in this, and even when unmarried women had babies, they could become "respectable" by marrying the baby's father.

Colonial law stated that a single woman could say the name of her baby's father while she was in labor, and the court would automatically believe her. This practice stemmed from the danger of dying in childbirth in a time before Cesarean surgical births were possible. In the deeply religious colonies, it was believed a woman would never lie before possibly meeting God.

**The First Conviction
for Abortion**

In the 1650s, William Mitchell was a respected member of the Maryland colony and served on the governor's council. His bondservant (similar to a slave) was a 21-year-old woman named Susan Warren. At some point, Mitchell either persuaded Warren to have sex with him, or he raped her. When Warren became pregnant, Mitchell forced her to drink a poison-ous concoction intended to induce abortion. She barely survived, and her baby was born dead.

According to court rec-ords, Mitchell was con-victed of "fornication, adultery, and murderous intention."[1] His penalty included a heavy fine, payable in tobacco, and removal from the gover-nor's council. Warren was whipped for fornication (illegal sex) but was freed from being Mitchell's bondservant.

If the father of the baby was already married, or unwilling to marry the mother, the couple faced disgrace. Although the father would be ordered to pay child support, many women were desperate to avoid dishonor. Unwed mothers stayed within the community, but they faced great shame. People sometimes turned to abortion in attempts to keep pregnancies secret.

In colonial times, surgical abortions were so dangerous, women almost never survived them. But many substances to bring about abortions were known. Depending on the amount used, these could accidentally kill both the mother and the fetus, kill only the fetus, or fail to work at all.

Although sex outside of marriage was forbidden in the colonies, abortion or infanticide (killing an infant) was considered the more serious crime. Numerous records exist of women and men punished for killing babies born to unmarried couples.

The 1800s

During the 1800s, American cities were growing. Many young people left their rural villages and traveled to cities in search of work. This trend had the side effect of removing many young people from the influence of their families. When single women became pregnant, there was now less pressure from the community for the issue to be resolved by marriage.

Although many churches opposed it, abortion was legal in most places in America during the nineteenth century. Midwives often prescribed herbs that would cause abortions, and advertisements for tonics that promised to cure "menstrual blockages" were common in publications of the time. American courts first took up the issue in 1812, in the *Commonwealth v. Bangs* case. In *Bangs*, the Massachusetts Supreme Court pronounced abortion legal, but only before quickening—the time when the mother could feel the fetus moving. At this point, society

Birth Control Declared Obscene

Anthony Comstock was an activist who, in 1873, headed an anti-vice campaign. His efforts ended in the so-called Comstock law, which banned the mailing of "obscene" materials. Under the federal law, birth control methods such as condoms also became illegal. Abortion-inducing drugs and advertisements for people who performed abortions were banned as well.

Some conservative Christian churches opposed birth control based on their interpretation of certain Bible passages. The religious groups believed sex was acceptable only if a married couple was trying to get pregnant. "Recreational" sex, with no intention of conceiving a child, was considered sinful even if the couple was married.

Today, some Christians still believe in this, but most now find birth control, especially within marriage, acceptable—if not essential.

had not addressed the question of the rights of the unborn. Laws were passed primarily to protect women's lives. Many women were injured or killed each year either by abortion-inducing drugs or by surgical abortions performed by inept folk healers.

THE ABORTION BAN

The American Medical Association (AMA) was established in 1847 and began organizing opposition to lay healers and herbalists who provided medical care. Herbalists competed with physicians for patients and were believed by the physicians to be incompetent. Although herbalists often provided safe care for minor problems, abortions remained dangerous, if not deadly, procedures. In response to an

1859 AMA resolution against abortion, state laws
began banning abortion. At this point in time, there
was no pro-life movement. Abortion was banned
mainly because it was unsafe. By 1890, abortion
was illegal throughout most of the United States.
However, despite a ban in Michigan, in 1882 doctors
in that state reported that 17 to 32 percent of all
pregnancies were still aborted.

THERAPEUTIC ABORTIONS

By 1900, abortion was illegal in all states except
Kentucky, though it was only allowed in cases when
it was necessary to maintain the life or health of the
mother. These special cases were called "therapeutic
abortions." However, it was up to the physician to
determine when an abortion was necessary. Some
doctors interpreted the law loosely, especially in cases
involving wealthy women or those with connections
in the medical profession.

Although abortion was illegal, enforcement of
the law was weak, and women were rarely brought to
trial. In 1904, a Chicago doctor reported that 10 to
13 percent of all pregnancies in the city were ending
in abortion.

ILLEGAL ABORTIONS

Birth control was unavailable in many areas during the early part of the twentieth century. Families were often large, and some mothers were overwhelmed by the number of children they had to care for. Women who married young and never used birth control could have 20 children. Sometimes even married women relied on abortion as a birth control method, despite the risks. Wealthier women could see doctors for "menstrual irregularities" (a term that really meant abortion), but many poor women died as a result of illegal abortions gone wrong.

Illegal abortions continued to be common throughout the century. Hospitals performed limited numbers of therapeutic abortions, but

Margaret Sanger

Comstock's law made birth control illegal in 1873. Birth control would continue to be illegal until the law was overturned in 1938. The change in law was due in large part to the efforts of a nurse named Margaret Sanger.

After seeing many poor women injured by abortions, Sanger began passing out pamphlets on birth control methods. She lobbied the Senate to change the law because she believed birth control would limit the use of abortion.

Sanger opened the first birth control clinic in 1916, an act for which she was sent to prison. Sanger is considered the founder of the Planned Parenthood Federation of America. She is also credited with coining the phrase *birth control*, which was called *voluntary motherhood* before her campaign.

Plastic models of fetuses are displayed as part of a Wisconsin congressman's testimony at a hearing about abortion bills in 1973.

many women could not afford proper medical care. Illegal abortions cost less but were performed by unqualified people under unclean conditions. Infections were common and sometimes deadly.

Some women tried to self-induce abortions. They usually did this by inserting a wire or some other sharp, narrow object, such as a coat hanger, into the cervix (opening from the vaginal canal into the uterus). These attempts often ended in death for the pregnant woman. Puncture wounds would spread bacteria into the blood, where they caused a deadly blood infection. If the injured woman received medical attention, she might have survived, but often with permanent reproductive problems. These disastrous outcomes were much more common before abortion became legal. That is why pro-choice rallies often feature women carrying signs with pictures of coat hangers and the slogan "never again."

MAKING ABORTION LEGAL

Beginning in 1967, some states legalized abortions under limited conditions, such as rape or incest, or if the pregnancy would damage the mother's health. Laws were made on a state-by-state basis, so what was legal in one state might be illegal in another. In 1969, the National Association for the Repeal of Abortion Laws lobbied individual states to decriminalize abortion. Abortion was not made legal in the United States on a federal level until the Supreme Court ruled on *Roe v. Wade.*

ROE V. WADE

The U.S. Supreme Court ruled on *Roe v. Wade* in 1973. The decision overturned all previous state laws regulating abortion. According to the federal law, abortions would be regulated based on the stage of the pregnancy. In the first trimester, or three months, all abortions are legal when performed by a doctor. Second-trimester abortions can be legally restricted so long as the mother's health is protected. Third-trimester abortions are likely to be denied, especially if the fetus is developed enough to survive outside the womb. The *Roe v. Wade* ruling allows third-trimester abortions only if it can be proved that allowing the pregnancy to go to term would endanger the mother.

Who Was Jane Roe?

The *Roe v. Wade* case was brought by a young woman from Texas named Norma McCorvey. To protect her privacy in this controversial case, she was called Jane Roe. Her opponent was Henry Wade, the Dallas County, Texas, district attorney.

When McCorvey became pregnant in 1969, she was a divorced mother of one daughter. She worked as a waitress and did not have the resources needed to raise a second child. She wanted an abortion, but Texas law stated that abortions were legal only if the pregnancy endangered the life of the mother. McCorvey was healthy, so she pretended she had been raped in an attempt to get the abortion approved. Her request was still denied. She later had a baby girl who was placed in an adoptive home. After this experience, she decided to take her case to court and try to overturn the law. As a result, abortion became legal throughout the United States in 1973. Since then, however, McCorvey has had a change of heart—today she is a spokesperson for the pro-life movement.

Opposition to *Roe v. Wade*

The 1973 *Roe v. Wade* decision was, and still is, very controversial. It triggered antiabortion demonstrations across the country. Pro-life activists want the decision overturned, but it has been upheld despite challenges in state and federal courts.

Medicaid is a federally funded program that provides health care to low-income Americans. After the *Roe v. Wade* decision, Medicaid paid for all abortions for a few years. In 1977, due to the efforts of pro-life Americans, federal funds for abortions were denied except in the cases of rape, incest, or danger to a woman's health. Antiabortion groups continued to work against funding for these exceptions. The health exception was removed in 1979, and exceptions for rape and incest followed in 1981. Medicaid funds no longer could be used for abortions—even if they were deemed medically necessary. Pro-choice activists opposed this rule and argued that it interfered with the right of poor women to obtain abortions. In 1993, the law was changed to again cover abortion in cases of incest, rape, or danger to the life of the woman. ⌒

Pro-life activists protest the Supreme Court's Roe v. Wade *decision on January 22, 1973.*

During the 1960s, hippies became a symbol of increasingly liberal attitudes about sex.

OUR CHANGING
SOCIETY

U.S. society has seen a trend of increasingly liberal views regarding sex. How have changing views on sex affected the debate on abortion?

Attitudes on Sex and Abortion in the 1950s

During the 1950s, sex was not discussed as openly as it is today. Teens were discouraged from kissing, and chaperones at social events were the norm. Birth control was difficult for young people to obtain. Without birth control, abstinence was the only way to avoid pregnancy. Teen pregnancies still occurred but were kept secret if possible.

It was considered important for a girl to remain a virgin until marriage. However, girls did not always comply with society's rules. A survey of women's magazines from the era shows that young women were taught to consider their virginity a commodity that should only be traded for the long-term security of a marriage. There were very limited employment opportunities for women, and most women were expected to become housewives. Those who did hold jobs made far less money than men, so many women could only achieve financial security through marriage.

In the 1950s, antibiotics became available to cure some sexually transmitted diseases (STDs), such as syphilis. STDs were often viewed as punishments for sin, and the availability of a cure set off a debate. Would removing the punishment for sex outside of marriage encourage people to become more sexually active? Would the institutions of marriage and family be threatened? The same questions would soon be raised about birth control and abortion.

Since all legal abortions were supposed to be therapeutic, hospitals limited the number of abortions they would perform. If an abortion was necessary to preserve the woman's health, she was often required to be made sterile to prevent her from ever getting pregnant again. Therapeutic abortions for poor women were denied more often than those for wealthy ones.

Redefining Therapeutic Abortion

In 1959, the American Law Institute (ALI), an association of judges and attorneys, proposed redefining therapeutic abortion. They believed it should include cases where a pregnancy would threaten not only the physical health of the mother, but also her mental health. Rape or incest and defects in the fetus were included as valid reasons for abortion.

Sex in the 1960s

Society in the 1960s went through some radical changes. Protests against the Vietnam War filled the streets. Women and people of color began demanding equal rights. Hippies believed in free love—the idea that there was nothing wrong with sex between unmarried people. Older and more conservative people tended to oppose these changes, leading to the "generation gap"—different opinions on social issues between the old and the young.

The invention of the birth control pill brought more social changes. The pill worked much better than other birth control methods, such as condoms, so women using the pill were very unlikely to become pregnant. For the first time, women were in control of whether or not they got pregnant. The invention of the birth control pill was controversial because many religious and socially conservative people believed it encouraged sex outside of marriage.

Despite the pill, many unintended pregnancies still ended in illegal abortions. Women often died as a result of illegal abortions, often performed by abortionists who were not doctors. The problem was worse

The Birth Control Pill

Birth control pills contain hormones, which are substances that naturally occur in the body to control its functions. Birth control pills usually contain a mixture of the female hormones estrogen and progesterone, but some pills only contain progesterone.

A woman cannot get pregnant when no eggs are released from her ovaries. When a woman takes the pill, ovulation, or the release of an egg, is prevented. Rarely, women who are on the pill do get pregnant, especially if they forget to take their daily pill. Birth control pills are available through doctors or through reproductive health care clinics, such as Planned Parenthood. The pill cannot prevent STDs, so doctors recommend that condoms be used as well. Abstinence is the only certain way to avoid pregnancy or STDs.

for women of color. In the early 1960s in New York City, one out of four childbirth-related deaths among white women was caused by abortion; but abortion caused half of such deaths among nonwhite women.

As a result of these deaths, and the widespread change in values, support for legal abortion began to increase.

THALIDOMIDE CAUSED BIRTH DEFECTS

Thalidomide was a drug that was available in Europe and Canada during the late 1950s and early 1960s. Though it was not sold in the United States, some American women were still able to obtain it. More than 10,000 women who took the drug during pregnancy to treat morning sickness or sleeplessness gave birth to deformed babies.

Some U.S. women who took thalidomide were allowed to obtain legal therapeutic abortions, but many others were not. The law still stipulated that abortions could only be performed if the mother's health was endangered. Behind closed doors, some surgeons interpreted the law more broadly. Many abortions were quietly performed to end pregnancies affected by thalidomide.

Thousands of deformed babies were still born, setting off intensified debate on the abortion issue. Some people felt that all babies should be born, no matter what. Others believed that the deformed children would suffer and possibly die, so it was kinder to abort them.

AMERICANS' VIEWS ON SEX TODAY

Americans generally have more liberal views on sex than ever before. There is a high rate of acceptance of single parents. A study published in 2007 reported that 95 percent of

Sherri Finkbine: A Reluctant Activist

In 1962, Sherri Finkbine was a local television personality in Arizona. A married mother of four, she was happily expecting her next child. When she discovered that the thalidomide she had taken while pregnant was likely to deform her baby, she went to her doctor. He recommended an abortion, and she agreed. Finkbine contacted the press, hoping to publicize the dangers of thalidomide. She did not want her name included in the article, but when it was published, she was identified. Although Finkbine had not intended to become an activist, the article set off a wave of national publicity and debate with her at the center.

Abortions were legal only to preserve the health of the mother and were not allowed in cases of deformity. The privacy that normally surrounded such matters often gave physicians the leeway to use their own judgment regarding abortions. Even so, hospitals performing abortions for thalidomide exposure were on shaky legal ground. The publicity surrounding Finkbine's case worried hospital administrators, who cancelled her abortion despite a court order allowing it to proceed. Unable to receive a legal abortion in the United States, Finkbine traveled to Sweden for the procedure. After the abortion, she and her husband learned that their baby was severely deformed and would not have survived.

AIDS, the Fatal STD

Sex is now riskier than it ever has been, due to HIV, the virus that causes AIDS. The HIV virus is primarily spread during sex but can also be passed when drug abusers share needles. Some STDs can be treated with antibiotics, but HIV is incurable. Expensive treatments delay the progression of the disease, but it is inevitably fatal.

The use of condoms reduces the chance of spreading the AIDS virus but does not completely eliminate the risk. About one-quarter of new HIV infections occur in people 21 and younger. Most of these young people do not know they are infected because they have no symptoms. HIV tests are available in any doctor's office or reproductive health care clinic.

Americans had sex before they were married.

Interestingly, more liberal views on sex and single parenthood do not necessarily extend to abortion. According to a 2007 Gallup poll, approximately 51 percent of Americans approve of keeping abortion legal.

The Debate Over the Morning-After Pill

Plan B is an emergency contraceptive often called the morning-after pill. Plan B is not an abortion pill to be taken by pregnant women. However, it can prevent a pregnancy if taken within 72 hours of sex. Approved by the U.S. Food and Drug Administration (FDA) in 2006, Plan B is now available at pharmacies to women 18 or older without a prescription.

In many ways, the approval of Plan B triggered the same debate as the birth control pill did. Some people approve of it because it is expected to prevent thousands of abortions. They point to a 2007 report that said use of emergency contraceptives in 2000 prevented approximately 100,000 unintended pregnancies and 51,000 abortions. Others disapprove because they feel it encourages extramarital or irresponsible sex.

Women under 18 can get Plan B, but only with a prescription. This age limit has created additional controversy. Advocates of Plan B protest that the delay involved in getting a prescription for a minor may make Plan B useless, as it only works for a short time after sex. Opponents of Plan B counter that permission slips are required before schools can even dispense aspirin, so minors should not receive any medication without the knowledge of their parents.

Emergency Contraception: Is It Abortion?

Emergency contraception reduces the risk of pregnancy by 89 percent if taken within three days of sex. Plan B contains hormones similar to those in the birth control pill. According to the FDA, the medicine inhibits ovulation. Therefore, it prevents a

pregnancy from ever occurring and does not induce an abortion.

Some pro-life advocates, including the National Conference of Catholic Bishops, disagree. They believe the pill may prevent conception but could also prevent a fertilized egg from implanting in the wall of the uterus. In their view, this is abortion because the fertilized egg is a potential person. Certain birth control methods, such as the IUD (intrauterine device), also prevent fertilized eggs from implanting. People who believe a fertilized egg should have human rights usually agree that IUDs are morally wrong, too.

Emergency Contraception

1 Take the first tablet as soon as possible within 72 hours of unprotected sex.

Emergency contraception known as Plan B can prevent a pregnancy if taken up to three days after unprotected sex.

Planned Parenthood workers, in orange, stand by to assist arriving clients past a group of pro-life protestors and into the clinic.

CONTROVERSY AND
DEMOCRACY

Social change in a democracy comes about when people persuade others to their point of view or when the views of the majority are written into law. Since agreement in the emotionally charged abortion debate is unlikely, conflict usually takes place through legislation, court battles, and street demonstrations. More rarely, impassioned individuals try to achieve their aims through illegal acts of violence and intimidation.

TACTICS OF ACTIVIST ORGANIZATIONS

Fundamentally, the abortion debate is a battle of ideas. Organizations make use of Web sites and printed publications to win people over to their point of view. Opinion, scientific evidence, and anecdotes all play a part in the debate. Advocates on both sides of the issue present information to play on the emotions of the reader.

Pro-life and pro-choice organizations raise funds to elect lawmakers who believe as they do. Lobbying is a major part of the activity of these organizations. Lobbyists might be private citizens advocating for an issue. Lobbyists can also be paid professionals hired

A Changing Supreme Court

Supreme Court judges serve for life. To protect the judges from political pressure, they cannot be removed from office and their salaries cannot be decreased during their term. New justices are appointed only if a current justice resigns or dies.

When a vacancy occurs on the U.S. Supreme Court, the president nominates a candidate. This candidate must then be confirmed by the U.S. Senate. During the Senate confirmation hearings, the nominated judge's stance on major issues, including abortion, is scrutinized.

Many pro-choice advocates feel that pro-life presidents and the Senate have nominated and confirmed more pro-life judges. These advocates fear the Supreme Court could overturn *Roe v. Wade*.

Wanda Franz, president of the NRLC, addresses the group's twenty-ninth annual convention in 2001.

by influential organizations. Elected officials are aware that their stance on issues must reflect those of the people who elected them. Otherwise, lawmakers cannot expect to remain in office.

MAJOR PRO-LIFE ORGANIZATIONS

Major pro-life organizations include the National Right to Life Committee (NRLC) and Birthright International. The NRLC opposes

euthanasia, or assisted suicide, as well as abortion.
The organization works toward legislative reform and
provides a "scorecard" reporting how elected officials
voted on important issues.

Birthright International works directly with
pregnant women, trying to encourage them not
to have abortions. The organization provides
counseling as well as maternity and baby clothes.
Unlike some crisis pregnancy centers, Birthright
does not attempt to influence women by showing
them graphic photographs of the abortion process.

Major Pro-choice Organizations

Two of the most prominent pro-choice
organizations are the Planned Parenthood
Federation of America and the National Abortion
Rights Action League (NARAL). Planned
Parenthood operates a network of clinics nationwide.
The clinics provide pregnancy tests and abortions.
They also treat STDs. Planned Parenthood also
provides birth control to minors without informing
the parents—a practice that has caused strong
opposition from conservative groups.

NARAL is primarily a political-action
organization working to influence elected officials.

NARAL encourages its members to lobby officials and publicize the issue in order to protect a woman's right to choose.

Crisis Pregnancy Centers

In 2007, there were an estimated 3,200 crisis pregnancy centers in the United States. These centers are run by pro-life organizations that counsel women with unintended pregnancies to avoid abortion. Crisis pregnancy centers have come under fire from pro-choice organizations. These critics argue that the crisis pregnancy centers masquerade as health care clinics but are staffed primarily with volunteers. In 1989, a Missouri woman successfully sued one center for refusing to share the results of her pregnancy test with her until she watched a disturbing antiabortion video.

Pro-life activists counter that the volunteers at these centers provide kind and nonjudgmental counseling. They counter that, far from being misleading, the centers provide scientifically accurate information about fetal development. Crisis pregnancy centers often use actual-size plastic models to show women what their fetuses look like at various stages of development. Some even offer free ultrasound examinations to view the fetus in the womb.

Due in part to the "compassionate conservatism" policy of President George W. Bush, these centers currently receive federal funding.

INVOLVEMENT OF CHURCHES

Christian churches have taken sides on both sides of the abortion debate. In general, Pentacostal and Evangelical churches tend to be pro-life, as are Mormons, Roman Catholics, and others. The list of pro-choice churches includes the Episcopals and Presbyterians, as well as many Jewish organizations. Most Muslim and Hindu scholars approve of legal abortion. Buddhists tend to disapprove of abortion, but most feel it should still be the woman's decision.

However, there is dissent within churches as well. For example, the Catholic Church threatened to excommunicate, or exclude, any member who had an abortion or helped someone else to do so. However, when polled privately, only 37 percent of U.S. Catholics said abortion was "always" wrong. A splinter group, Catholics for a Free Choice, advocates for choice in the abortion decision.

FREEDOM OF SPEECH OR HARASSMENT?

The First Amendment of the U.S. Constitution guarantees the right to free speech and assembly. But where does free speech end and harassment begin? Many people agree that physical confrontations should

The FACE Act

The Freedom of Access to Clinic Entrances (FACE) Act makes it illegal to harass anyone trying to enter a reproductive health care clinic. Under the act, physical obstruction, intimidation, or use of force against clinic patients are federal crimes. The FACE Act was signed by President Bill Clinton in 1994. Between 1994 and 2005, 71 people were convicted for FACE violations. Clinic violence has declined since the act was passed. In 1994, 52 percent of clinics reported incidents of "severe violence," including bombings, stalking, death threats, and murder. After the passage of FACE, only 20 percent of clinics reported such problems.

FACE does not interfere with First Amendment free speech laws. Abortion protestors may still peacefully picket clinics and hand out literature.

be illegal, but the issue of verbal communication is more difficult to categorize. For example, do pro-life activists have the right to confront women entering clinics where abortions are provided?

Pro-life groups believe that this behavior falls under their right of free speech, but pro-choice groups view it as a form of harassment.

NOW v. Scheidler

The National Organization for Women (NOW) filed *NOW v. Scheidler* in response to widespread antiabortion demonstrations. The class-action lawsuit represented several abortion clinics as well as their patrons. In the suit, NOW alleged that the pro-life activists Joseph Scheidler of Operation Rescue and Pro-Life Action League leaders Timothy Murphy and Andrew Scholberg were "coordinating violent attacks against abortion providers."[1]

In 1998, the three men were found guilty of organizing a nationwide campaign to intimidate employees and patients at abortion clinics. They were ordered to pay a judgment of almost $300,000. The men were not implicated in any individual acts of violence.

DEMONSTRATIONS BY PRO-LIFE GROUPS

Some pro-life groups organize loud demonstrations outside abortion clinics. In a technique called "sidewalk counseling," demonstrators carry photographs of aborted fetuses. Or they approach individual women trying to enter the clinic. Some activists only talk to the women and hand out antiabortion literature. Others shout and make strong accusations, or they physically block women from leaving their cars or entering the clinic. Occasionally these confrontations escalate into violence, with personal and property damage on both sides.

Pro-life activists also stage disruptive demonstrations at the homes of abortion providers. Sometimes bullhorns are used to amplify their voices as they chant antiabortion slogans. Some abortion providers have been intimidated into quitting their jobs by such tactics.

Violence against Abortion Providers

The National Abortion Federation compiles statistics on incidents of clinic violence by antiabortion extremists. Between 1977 and 2007, seven abortion providers were murdered. There were also 41 bombings and 162 counts of assault and battery. As a result, the abortion clinics have instituted safety measures including security guards, bulletproof glass, security cameras, and staff outfitted with bulletproof vests.

Two antiabortion groups, Operation Rescue and the Pro-Life Action League, organized clinic protests. Joseph Scheidler, the leader of Operation Rescue, spoke out against the use of violence in his book, *Closed: 99 Ways to Stop Abortion*. Operation Rescue asks protestors to pledge they will "be peaceful and non-violent in word and deed."[2] However, Operation Rescue cofounder Joe Foreman once signed a statement that read, "The use of lethal force is justified if it is carried out for the purpose of protecting the lives of unborn children."[3] Another Operation Rescue activist, Michael Bray, agreed with Foreman, saying assassination was a "rational way of following the Operation Rescue dictum: 'If you believe abortion is murder, then act like it.'"[4]

Violence against Pro-life Activists

Although clinic violence has been well publicized, pro-life extremists are by no means the only ones committing illegal acts of violence and harassment. The Bowie-Crofton Pregnancy Clinic in Bowie, Maryland, encourages women to consider alternatives to abortion. In 2005, the clinic was severely vandalized. Windows were broken and pro-choice messages were spray-painted on the walls.

Pro-life activists have reported numerous incidents of threats and damage to their vehicles. The incidents have occurred primarily during demonstrations or sidewalk counseling.

James E. Kopp, a longtime associate of Operation Rescue founder Randall Terry, was convicted for the 1998 murder of Buffalo abortion doctor Barnett A. Slepian.

Pro-life and pro-choice activists demonstrate on the steps of the U.S. Supreme Court after a 1989 ruling that gave states increased power to limit abortions.

THE GRAY ZONE

Many special circumstances affect the abortion debate. Do the ethics of abortion change if the fetus has a defect or a disease? What if the mother was a drug abuser and the baby would be born brain damaged and addicted?

What if the pregnancy resulted from rape? The situation appears simple to people who are strong pro-choice or pro-life supporters, but others feel the circumstances surrounding the decision for an abortion matter. To people in this gray zone, some abortions are morally right and others are wrong.

PREGNANCIES RESULTING FROM RAPE

The NOW reports that 32,000 rape victims become pregnant by their attackers every year in the United States. Pro-life advocates refer to these pregnancies as "hard cases" because a higher proportion of people feel abortion is acceptable in cases of rape. The pro-life organization Right to Life of Michigan opposes abortions in rape cases, stating,

> *Despite the common misconception that aborting the fetus will alleviate the trauma of rape, often quite the opposite is true. Abortion in rape cases frequently only compounds the psychological duress experienced by the victim.*[1]

Many rape victims disagree. They feel that being forced to deliver the child of their attacker would be cruel, and that abortion is important to their healing process. These women contend that they would apply their feelings about the rapist to the child and could not be good mothers for those babies.

Rape victims may also arrange for an adoption of the baby. More rarely, they choose to keep the baby. It is becoming more common for such mothers to come forward with their stories and be open with their children about their origins.

NARAL Pro-Choice America advocates for emergency contraception to be offered to every rape victim. Catholic-run hospitals do not usually offer this option, creating controversy.

Prenatal Testing

Prenatal testing is a general term for a variety of tests that can be done to check the health of a fetus. Prenatal testing can detect the presence of many inherited disorders. Down syndrome, Duchenne muscular dystrophy,

Colorado Rape Contraception Law

In March of 2007, Colorado Governor Bill Ritter signed into law an act requiring all hospitals in the state to provide information about the availability of emergency contraception to rape victims. The law contains measures to accommodate differing ethical viewpoints on medication. Catholic hospitals, which are opposed to it, are bound by the law to convey information about where emergency contraception can be obtained. They do not need to provide the medication themselves. Under the law, employees who are opposed to emergency contraception are not required to recommend it, as another staff person will do so.

sickle-cell anemia, and Tay-Sachs disease are just some of the disorders that can be diagnosed by prenatal testing.

Although most pregnant women take advantage of some form of prenatal testing, the practice is controversial because of its connection to abortion. Some argue that letting parents know if the fetus is defective opens the door to abortion. Others contend that parents deserve the right to know so they can be prepared for the special needs of their baby.

Prenatal Testing

There are three general types of prenatal tests: blood sampling from the mother, amniocentesis, and chorionic villus sampling.

Blood tests are usually taken at a pregnant woman's first visit to her doctor. The tests provide information on the mother's blood type and her exposure to diseases that could threaten her baby.

Amniocentesis is the removal of a small amount of amniotic fluid (the fluid surrounding the fetus in the uterus) through a needle. This test occurs during the fourth month of pregnancy. Doctors pass the needle through the mother's abdomen while watching the fetus through ultrasound. This minimizes the chance of poking the fetus with the needle. Amniotic fluid contains cells from the fetus and can be used for genetic tests. Amniocentesis can reveal more than 150 disorders, including Down syndrome and Tay-Sachs disease.

Chorionic villus sampling (CVS) is another way to obtain fetal cells. CVS can be performed using a tiny tube inserted into the vagina and through the cervix. Doctors can also insert a long needle through the abdomen to obtain the cells. A tiny portion of the membranes surrounding the fetus is removed. CVS can be done more than two months earlier in the pregnancy than amniocentesis and reveals similar information about a fetus.

ABORTION OF SPECIAL-NEEDS BABIES

Researchers work to develop methods of detecting disorders earlier in pregnancies, since abortions are safer and less traumatic in the first trimester. People tend to find abortion more acceptable in cases of fetal abnormality, and many parents choose abortion in such cases. They reason that the disabled child would have a poor quality of life, and his or her special needs would place great emotional and financial strain on a family.

Duchenne Muscular Dystrophy

Duchenne muscular dystrophy is an inherited disease that almost always affects boys. It can be detected by prenatal testing. The disease causes muscles to progressively weaken until the child can no longer walk. The disease begins with weakness in the legs, frequent falls, and poor coordination. Generally, by the age of 12, the boy is confined to a wheelchair. Affected men usually die by age 25.

For example, Tay-Sachs disease is a fatal inherited condition. Babies born with this genetic disorder appear normal at first, but deteriorate mentally and physically. Generally, they do not live more than four years. Many couples choose to terminate Tay-Sachs pregnancies because the children cannot be saved.

This trend is opposed by pro-life advocates who believe that all children, not just healthy ones, deserve to be born. In their view, society should work to cure the diseases, not prevent the births of those who are afflicted with them. The pro-life Canadian Centre for Bio-Ethical Reform asserts that "people with limitations have a right to life just like so-called 'normal' or healthy people."[2]

DOWN SYNDROME BABIES

Down syndrome is a form of mild to moderate retardation. People with Down syndrome are short in stature and have almond-shaped eyes and flattened profiles. Symptoms and degrees of functioning range from moderate to severe. There is no cure for Down syndrome. Some people with the syndrome can hold simple jobs and live independently with little help. Others never learn to talk and may require almost constant supervision.

In 2005, a test became available that would identify 95 percent of Down syndrome babies in their first

Sickle-Cell Anemia

Sickle-cell anemia is an inherited disease that mostly affects African Americans. The disease causes red blood cells, which carry oxygen, to become misshapen. Usually red blood cells are round. If they "sickle," they become curved like crescent moons. This curved shape looks like an old-fashioned farm tool called the sickle.

The curved red blood cells hook onto each other and become lodged in small blood vessels, causing painful blockages. The blockages usually occur when oxygen is low in the body, such as during exercise or when traveling at high altitude. Sickled red blood cells are gradually destroyed by the body, causing a shortage of red blood cells. A person low on red blood cells is anemic, and they often feel weak and tire more easily.

A father reads with his daughter, who has Down syndrome.

trimester of development. The early Down syndrome test gives parents the option of aborting and trying again for a normal baby. Currently, approximately 80 percent of babies with Down syndrome are being aborted in the United States.

Couples or single mothers must decide whether they have the emotional and financial resources to care for their vulnerable child. Most decide that they do not. The emotional and financial investment is long-term, as parents often support Down syndrome children through adulthood. People with Down syndrome do have shortened lives, but they will still likely outlive their parents. Later in life, the elderly parents must make arrangements for the care of their special-needs adult.

Most people with Down syndrome have cheerful, loving personalities and clearly enjoy their lives. Although they do sometimes have heart and lung problems, they do not suffer on a daily basis. This fact has heightened the controversy regarding the abortion of Down syndrome babies.

The abortion trend concerns parents of children with Down syndrome. Will their efforts to mainstream their children into normal classrooms be set back if the condition becomes rare? Many Down syndrome people are capable of understanding that they are different and feel isolated. Best Buddies is an organization that fosters friendships among people with mental disabilities. Its founder, Anthony Shriver, said that for Down syndrome children "loneliness is one of the most significant challenges they face, and it would only become more acute as they became a smaller segment of the population."[3]

Effect of Special-needs People on Society

Society recognizes that caring for disabled children can be a burden, but it can also be a benefit. We learn compassion from disabled children while admiring their determination to overcome obstacles. We learn how to be comfortable with people who are different from ourselves. Most parents hope their children will be born perfect and whole, but collectively, would we want a society of only perfect people?

What will be the long-term effect on society if most disabled children are never born? Fewer families would go through the strain of caring for a special-needs child. Costs of care would decline. Yet, with fewer advocates for them, government-financed programs to benefit special-needs people would probably decline. What would life be like for the remaining differently abled individuals in the world? —

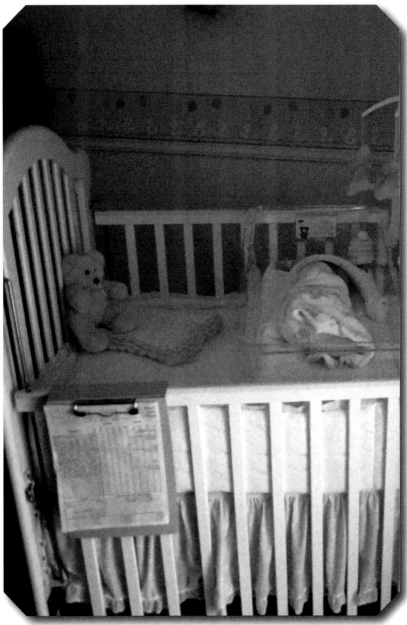

A newborn baby is addicted to the drugs her mother took while pregnant.
At a pediatric care center, the infant is kept in a dark, quiet place to avoid
over stimulation.

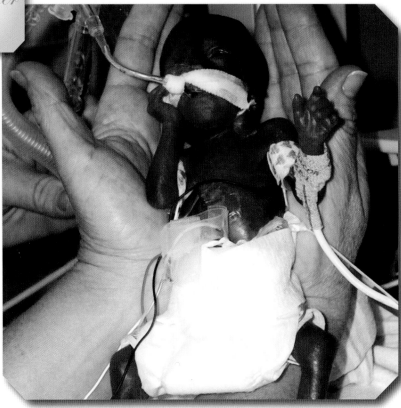

Amillia Sonja Taylor, born more than three months early in 2006, is the earliest premature baby to ever survive.

SHIFTING BOUNDARIES

Advances in medical technology change our perceptions about the boundaries of "viability," the age at which a preterm infant can survive outside the womb. *Roe v. Wade* passed in 1973. At that time, premature babies almost never survived if they were born before 24 weeks of gestation. The *Roe v. Wade* decision did not mandate a specific number of weeks as the point at which states may legally protect the fetus. It set that point at "approximate viability," though, even then, it insisted that protecting the mother's health was an overriding consideration. However, preterm babies as young as 22 weeks now can survive, although their rate of disability is high. What does it mean now that "approximate viability" is earlier? For example, does *Roe v. Wade* require that special care be given to protect preterm newborns?

Roe v. Wade still permits late-term abortions in the United States when they are performed for compelling reasons, such as to protect the health of the mother. Still, medical advances have made many people question the ethics of the 24-week limit. Pro-life advocates point out that it is legal for

The Earliest Premature Baby to Survive

The earliest premature baby to survive was born in October 2006 at just 22 weeks of gestation. Amillia Sonja Taylor was 9.5 inches (24 cm) long and weighed less than 10 ounces (283 g) at birth. The baby was delivered early by Cesarean be-cause her mother had complications with the pregnancy. Baby Amillia spent four months in a Miami hospital.

Challenges of Preterm Infants

Risk of death or disability of a premature infant increases the earlier the baby is born. Premature babies are cared for by specialists in neonatal intensive care units of hospitals.

Because the earliest preterm infants cannot nurse, they are fed through a needle inserted into a vein. Premature babies who survive have a high rate of long-term problems such as mental disabilities, cerebral palsy, blindness, deafness, and digestive or breathing problems.

a 23-week-old premature baby to be cared for in a hospital's neonatal intensive care unit, while another 23-week-old fetus is aborted. This is a difficult issue for pro-choice people as well. Many do not want to see the law changed because they fear it would be the beginning of a slippery slope in which abortion rights would gradually be eroded.

VIABILITY TESTING BEFORE ABORTION?

The lungs of a fetus are not inflated and will not inflate until the baby takes its first breath. To keep delicate, damp lung tissue from sticking together, our bodies produce a substance called surfactant. Surfactant is not produced in fetal lungs until approximately the sixth month of pregnancy. Exactly when surfactant is produced varies

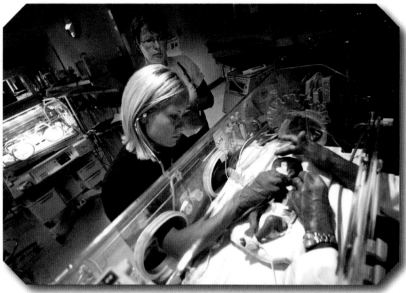

Medical professionals attend to a premature infant at a neonatal intensive care unit.

between individual babies. If a premature baby does not produce enough surfactant, it will have trouble breathing. Respiratory difficulty is the leading cause of death among preterm infants.

In a situation where the pregnancy threatens the mother's health, doctors may recommend a late-term abortion. To avoid aborting a fetus that could survive on its own, some people advocate testing for viability. In large part, a viability test determines if the fetus has begun producing surfactant. Medical professionals point out that surfactant is not the only factor that influences whether a preterm infant will survive. Birth weight and the general health of the infant are also major influences on the survival rate. Some states now require viability testing before late-term abortions.

Partial-birth Abortions

In 1996, Congress voted to ban a form of late-term abortion sometimes called partial-birth abortion. This medical "intact dilation and extraction" procedure occurs in the third trimester of pregnancy. The fetus is partially removed from the womb before it is aborted.

Though Congress passed the bill, President Bill Clinton vetoed it. He said it went too far in banning partial-birth abortion even when the fetus was severely disabled or when a woman's health was threatened. After Clinton's veto, more than 30 states enacted their own laws banning the procedure. President Bush signed the Partial Birth Abortion Ban Act of 2003 into law. In two landmark cases, the Supreme Court upheld the law in 2007. For pro-life advocates, this signaled a key victory. For the first time since *Roe v. Wade,* the Supreme Court permitted a ban on an abortion procedure.

Babies That Survive Abortions

A ten-year British study, completed in 2007, reported that one in thirty late-term abortions of disabled fetuses resulted in the live birth of a baby.

Most of these infants died within a few hours. This raised a dilemma for doctors, who feared being accused of murder if the baby was born alive and then died. Pro-life activists take a great interest in this study. Since it included only cases in which the fetus had a disability, they raise the question of how many normal babies must have survived abortions.

Survivors of Abortion

An American woman named Gianna Jessen is an adult today, but was born as a survivor of an abortion. Her 17-year-old mother was seven months pregnant when she decided to have the abortion. The doctor injected saline solution into the uterus, which was expected to kill the fetus. Jessen's young mother waited at the abortion clinic, but the predicted contractions did not begin. The abortion provider left the office that evening, leaving the young woman in the care of the night nurse. That night Jessen was born alive, weighing only two pounds (0.9 kg). The nurse transferred her to an emergency medical clinic. Jessen survived but suffers from cerebral palsy. She now campaigns for pro-life issues.

Other infants who survive abortion are so severely damaged that they do not make it to adulthood. Sarah Brown was blinded and disabled as a result of an abortion attempt in the seventh month of gestation. The abortionist's needle pierced the base of her skull and her head above the eye, injecting a toxic substance. Brown survived and was placed in an adoptive family. She never walked or talked and died at age five from brain damage caused during the abortion.

THE BORN-ALIVE INFANTS PROTECTION ACT

The care of infants who have survived abortions, or born-alive infants, was addressed in the Born-Alive Infants Protection Act, signed into law by President Bush in 2002. The act ensured that any living infant, regardless of whether the birth occurred as a result of abortion, be given full human rights. Before the act was passed, hospital policies varied. In most cases, born-alive infants were given "comfort care." For example, they were placed in a warm incubator and given oxygen, but no further measures were taken to keep them alive. Other hospitals treated born-alive infants like any other premature babies and placed them in neonatal intensive care. A wave of negative publicity resulted from revelations that

Costs and Ethics of the Born-Alive Infants Protection Act

Premature babies may spend months in the hospital, and the hospital bills can reach a million dollars or more. Laws that mandate intensive care for born-alive infants mean that unwanted infants could be treated in the hospital at enormous expense. Who should pay the bills—the hospital, taxpayers, or the parents of the aborted infant? If the infant should survive, he or she may suffer and most likely be disabled.

Also, finding adoptive homes for disabled children is difficult. Some argue that it is more ethical to let such infants die, but others believe every baby deserves a chance.

certain abortion clinics gave such infants no care at all. Most born-alive infants die because they are too premature, but a few have survived.

Do Fetuses Feel Pain?

At eight weeks of gestation, a fetus will turn away from a touch. Does this prove they can feel touch and, therefore, feel pain? Do fetuses feel pain when they are aborted?

A 2005 study by a team of doctors reported that fetuses probably cannot feel pain before about 29 weeks of development. For pain to be felt, a nerve pathway must be complete between the body and the brain. When this pathway is incomplete, reflexes exist, but true pain is not possible.

Pro-life advocates often disagree. They point out that the behavior of premature infants provides a clue to the experience of fetuses. Tubes and needles must be inserted into premature infants to help them breathe and eat. The infants may cry or recoil from these unpleasant sensations. It is difficult to determine if these responses are reflexes or true pain.

This debate is important because some states are considering legislation that would require doctors to inform women seeking abortions that the fetus may feel pain and offer pain medication for the fetus. Painkillers are currently available for the fetus during abortions, but some doctors believe these drugs increase the risk to the mother. Some pain medications may increase bleeding in the uterus.

President George W. Bush signed the Born-Alive Infants Protection Act into law in August 2002.

A baby girl in a Chinese orphanage could likely be adopted by U.S. parents.

ABORTION ON THE
INTERNATIONAL SCENE

The highest abortion rate in the world, 90 per 1,000 women, is in Eastern Europe, where poverty rates are high and social problems are severe. By comparison, the abortion rate in North America was 22 per 1,000 women in 1996.

Throughout South America, abortion is either illegal or allowed only to save the mother's life. In Chile, women can be imprisoned for having an illegal abortion. The situation is similar in most African nations. Abortion is legal throughout most of Eastern and Western Europe, with the exception of Ireland. It is also legal in most Asian countries.

CHINA'S ONE-CHILD POLICY

China's population is estimated at more than 1.3 billion, about one-fifth of the planet's total people. China's government encourages, or even forces, abortion to control its overpopulation problem.

Overpopulation has caused severe pollution and an alarming depletion of natural resources in the country. Also, when people are overcrowded and sanitation is poor, the risk of starvation or disease is high. Desperate to control the situation, China's government instituted a one-child-per-family policy in 1979.

Abortions Worldwide

Each year, 40 million abortions are performed around the world. Of these, 20 million are performed illegally. An estimated 78,000 deaths occur each year as a result of illegal abortions, which are often performed in unsafe conditions. That number accounts for approximately one in seven pregnancy-related deaths worldwide. In some African countries where abortion is illegal, abortions count for as many as half of all pregnancy-related deaths. In countries where abortion is legal, they cause less than 1 percent of all deaths related to pregnancy.

The Chinese government has more control over people's personal lives than do governments in Western countries. Although the one-child policy is very unpopular, the Chinese people have no choice about cooperating. Powerful officials of the Chinese Family Planning Office regulate marriage licenses and permits to have children. Women must wait to marry until age 20 and men until 22. Births by single women are prohibited. If a single woman does become pregnant, family

---

Abortion Ethics and World Population Growth

As of 2007, the world's population is more than 6.7 billion people and is expected to grow by almost half again by 2050. The planet is in the midst of the worst mass extinction of plants and animals in 67 million years. This extinction is largely caused by humans. Growing cities spread concrete over the land, wiping out natural populations of plants and animals. Humans also take part in ecosystems. Since we depend on other life forms to survive, loss of species increases our own risk of eventual extinction.

Overpopulation is also causing damage to our planet, which will take hundreds or thousands of years to heal. Pollution, erosion of soils, global warming, and damage to our protective ozone layer are only a few examples of human-caused harm. This damage is reducing the total number of people that Earth can support. A decline in population seems inevitable, whether through careful planning by governments or by uncontrolled war, famine, and disease.

Pro-choice advocates argue that, considering the immense problems of overpopulation, abortion is the most ethical choice society can make for unwanted pregnancies. Pro-life activists counter that abortion is never ethical, no matter the circumstances.

planning officials usually force her to have an abortion. Human rights activists worldwide have opposed this practice, especially because some of the abortions occur within weeks of delivery.

During the 1990s, the regulations were relaxed to some extent. Urban couples were still only allowed one child. Rural couples, who needed children to work on farms, sometimes were allowed two or three children. Families could often pay a fine or bribe a corrupt official and be allowed to keep an extra, "unregistered" child. Unregistered children had few prospects for education or employment because they lacked the required documents. These children usually became second-class citizens.

Two Extremes

In Canada, abortions are permitted at any time during a pregnancy and for any reason, though many physicians are still reluctant to perform late-term abortions. In the South American countries of Nicaragua and El Salvador, abortion is always illegal, even in cases when abortion would save the life of the mother.

Sex-selection Abortions

Chinese families prefer sons to daughters for several reasons. Boys have higher status in China, just as the men have higher status than women. Additionally, first-born sons in China take responsibility for their parents when the parents grow old, while girls traditionally care for elderly in-laws. Parents of sons usually feel more secure that they will be taken care of when they are old.

Because of the strict limit on family size and the preference for boys, abortion is used in China as a method for selecting the sex of the child. Many couples who are expecting babies go to clinics where ultrasound is used to detect the gender of the fetus. Female fetuses are more likely to be aborted if the parents already have one or more daughters, since families become increasingly desperate to produce a son. Not all expectant parents get ultrasound, of course, and many are not willing to abort even if the baby is a girl.

Still, gender ratios in China are now skewed. There are now 120 boys for every 100 girls in

Is the Status of Chinese Women Improving?

Today, many young Chinese women are cherished only children. A lone daughter is often treated as the family once treated the valued sons. Especially in cities, solitary daughters are lavished with education and love. These girls grow up with high self-esteem that was probably rare in their mothers' generation. Many are postponing marriage and focusing on their careers. When they do marry, they are choosing wealthier, better educated husbands who treat them as equals.

China. By comparison, a normal sex ratio is between 103 and 105 boys for every 100 girls.

In 2003, China outlawed abortion for sex selection. However, illegal mobile clinics reportedly continue to provide low-cost sex scanning and abortions.

SEX-SELECTION ABORTIONS IN INDIA

Like China, India has a societal preference for boys. Girls are more expensive to raise, and they become part of their husband's household at marriage. Families are obligated to pay for traditional rituals for girls as they grow. When a girl marries, her parents must provide a dowry, which is a payment of cash or valuables to the groom's family.

Although overpopulation is a problem in India, it has no family-size limit like China. India still has one of the most skewed gender ratios in the world: 927 females to every 1,000 males. Abortion is

George W. Bush Restricts International Aid

In 2001, U.S. President George W. Bush decided that taxpayer money would no longer be awarded to international aid agencies that provided abortions or information on abortions. Under the Clinton administration, federal funding had been provided to such agencies. The decision was applauded by pro-life organizations but opposed by the World Health Organization.

legal in India, but abortion for gender selection is not. Laws prohibit health care providers from even revealing a fetus's gender. Still, ultrasound machines are common, and there is a thriving underground business in tests that reveal a fetus's gender.

SOCIAL EFFECTS OF UNEQUAL GENDER RATIOS

Some political scientists fear that a surplus of young men in India and China may lead to increasing social problems. In their view, women are a stabilizing influence on society, and men with no prospects for relationships are more likely to form gangs and commit crimes. Crime rates indeed have risen in areas of India with the fewest women. A few researchers have even suggested that wars may become more likely, as governments try to find a way to keep restless young men off the streets.

An Indian girl looks out over the crowd during an event to oppose sex-selection abortions in New Delhi, India, in 2006.

A mother cries while hugging her pregnant 13-year-old daughter in Knoxville, Tennessee.

ABORTION AND FAMILIES

bortion affects not only the mother and her fetus, but her family and male partner as well. If the pregnant woman chooses abortion, the baby's father lost a child he might have wanted. The young couple's parents lost a grandchild they might have wanted. Who should have a say in the choice to abort a pregnancy?

Conversely, what if the pregnancy is upsetting to the family, and they want it hidden by a quick and quiet abortion? Should family members have a right to mandate an abortion? Sometimes girls as young as 10 or 12 become pregnant. Should parents be able to schedule an abortion for a very young daughter? Parental consent laws are the product of such debates.

ARGUMENTS IN FAVOR OF PARENTAL CONSENT LAWS

In some states, parental consent laws require that pregnant teens notify their parents before having an abortion. Parental consent laws might require that after a girl tells her parents, she must wait a certain amount of time before the abortion is allowed. The waiting period is intended to give the family time to discuss the situation and come to a decision.

Those in favor of parental consent laws believe that loving parents want to know what their daughters are going through so they can help. They believe abortion is too major of a decision for a minor to make without support. Both pro-choice and pro-life

William Bell: An Opponent of Parental Consent Laws

Becky Bell, a 16-year-old pregnant teen from Indiana, died from an illegal abortion in 1988. The state of Indiana had a parental consent law, and Becky chose to have an illegal abortion rather than inform her parents. Her parents believe she was afraid of disappointing them, so she kept her pregnancy a secret. Becky's father, William Bell, has since become an activist against laws that require teens to notify their parents before having an abortion.

advocates may support parental consent laws.

There are sound medical reasons for parents to be notified. After an abortion, a girl is at risk for infection or she may experience bleeding, even if the abortion was properly performed. These problems can be life threatening and require immediate medical care. If the parents did not know about their daughter's abortion, serious symptoms could be overlooked.

THE CASE AGAINST TELLING PARENTS

People who are opposed to parental consent laws point out that many teens do not want to tell their parents that they are pregnant. These girls would go out of state or even seek illegal abortions to avoid family confrontations. Girls might keep a secret because they are afraid of hurting their parents, or they might want an abortion but know their parents would not approve. Children of emotionally abusive or violent parents may be frightened not knowing how their parents may respond. In these cases, parental consent laws block a girl's access to a safe and legal abortion.

JUDICIAL BYPASS AVOIDS PARENTAL CONSENT

In some states that require parental consent, a pregnant teen can obtain a judicial bypass to avoid obtaining her parents' consent for an abortion. A judicial bypass is awarded by a judge in a court. The judge allows an exception to the parental consent law if the girl can demonstrate that she has given

A Judicial Bypass

A minor who wants a judicial bypass can contact the National Abortion Federation, American Civil Liberties Union (ACLU), or Planned Parenthood for guidance. Local branches of these organizations can be located online or in the telephone book. Planned Parenthood clinics provide service on a sliding scale, so poor people pay a very low fee. Often teens are not from poor families but have little money of their own. Such girls are usually charged very low fees.

The clinic will perform an ultrasound to verify the girl is pregnant. The girl also will receive counseling on options such as abortion, adoption, or keeping the baby. The clinic will not telephone the girl's home, send mail, or inform anyone of the situation. If the minor has reason to expect violence in her home if her pregnancy were revealed, she would be advised to keep all documents from the clinic and counselor in a safe place.

Next, the girl needs to go to the courthouse and fill out a form. She will be appointed a free attorney to guide her through the process. If she receives the judicial bypass and still wants the abortion, documents from the court will authorize it. Typically, this process takes only a few days.

informed consent to the abortion procedure and is mature enough to make the decision. "Informed consent" means that the young woman has been educated about the abortion procedure, its consequences, and its associated risks. The judge must also decide that it is in her best interest to have the abortion without telling her parents. For example, if the judge felt the minor risked abuse if her parents were informed, he or she would award her a judicial bypass. The girl would then be provided with documents authorizing the abortion.

GRANDPARENTS' RIGHTS

Parents of a pregnant teen are the grandparents of that fetus, and they might have strong protective feelings about it. In states with parental consent laws, teens' parents can block them from having abortions. It is not unusual for parents who oppose a daughter's abortion to help raise their grandchild. This option keeps the baby in the family and allows the young mother to continue her schooling and social life.

If a girl chooses to give birth rather than have an abortion, her baby's grandparents may have some legal rights. This includes the grandparents who are

the parents of a man whom she may
no longer have a relationship with.
In some states, grandparents can
successfully sue for rights to visit their
grandchild, even over the opposition
of one or both of the baby's parents.

Men's Rights

In the abortion debate, the father
of the fetus is frequently forgotten.
Should a man be able to legally
force a woman to carry his child
to term if she does not want to be
pregnant? Should a man who does
not want to become a father be able
to legally force the mother to have an
abortion?

Men often have strong feelings
about the issue. Sometimes a
pregnancy is unplanned, and the
man feels he cannot afford to pay
child support. These men have
argued that since they do not want the
baby, they should not be responsible
for its support. In other cases, a man

Man Loses Suit to Stop Abortion

When John Stachokus and his girlfriend Tanya Meyers broke up in 2002, she was already pregnant with his child. She decided to have an abortion, and he went to the courts to stop her. He won a rare, if brief, victory. An order from a Pennsylvania judge temporarily blocked the abortion until the case could be heard. A week later Stachokus lost his case. "Neither an ex-boyfriend nor a fetus has a standing to interfere with a woman's choice to terminate her pregnancy," said the judge.[1]

An 18-year-old father cares for his young daughter at home in Des Moines, Iowa.

very much wants his child, but the woman refuses to carry the fetus to term. Those men, who already think of themselves as fathers, mourn the loss of their children.

Courts have consistently ruled that women's rights take precedence over men's rights where pregnancies are concerned. In the United States, at least a dozen cases have gone to court in which men tried to block women from having abortions. In all cases, the men have lost, and the Supreme Court has refused to hear their appeals. Taking a case to the Supreme Court can take years, and abortion decisions must be made within weeks. But these cases do set a precedent.

Two key court cases are the 1976 ruling in *Danforth v. Planned Parenthood* and the 1992 *Planned Parenthood v. Casey.* In *Danforth,* the Supreme Court overruled a provision in a Missouri law that required a married woman to provide the written consent of her husband before having an abortion. The decision was reaffirmed in *Casey.* In that case, the Supreme Court struck down a Pennsylvania ruling ordering married women to inform their husbands before getting abortions.

No Forced Abortions

A man is not legally allowed to demand that his wife or girlfriend have an abortion. If a woman bears a man's child, he must pay child support whether or not he wants the

If the Identity of the Father Is Uncertain

If a woman had sex with more than one man within the month she became pregnant, she cannot be sure who is the father of the baby. Paternity tests determine if a certain man is the father of a child or not. The tests can be done while the woman is pregnant (prenatal paternity testing) or after the baby is born. Prenatal paternity testing can be done as early as ten weeks gestation, which still allows the couple to make a decision for or against abortion.

If a woman names a man as the father of her child and he denies it, a paternity test can be ordered by the court. If that man is indeed the father, he will be ordered to pay child support to the mother of his baby. Unless the father has a record of criminal behavior or abuse, he is likely to receive visitation rights to spend time with his child.

baby. This is true even if the couple was not married or in a relationship when the woman became pregnant.

Abusive men have been known to bully their pregnant wives or girlfriends into having abortions. Before the procedure, a woman can privately notify abortion clinic staff if she does not want to have an abortion. The clinic staff would not perform an unwanted abortion and can help an abused woman find free shelter at a safe house for battered women.

Parents of a pregnant teen might urge her to have an abortion, but they also cannot legally force her to have one. This is true no matter how young the pregnant girl may be. Girls who fear abuse from parents can legally seek shelter by informing clinic staff.

An intake worker at an abortion clinic checks in a teenage
client in San Francisco, California.

Demonstrators on opposing sides of the debate react to a new antiabortion law in South Dakota in March 2006.

PSYCHOLOGICAL EFFECTS
OF ABORTION

Evidence on the psychological effects of abortion is mixed. This is probably because the long-term mental and emotional effects depend on the individual woman and the circumstances surrounding her abortion.

Pro-life Perspective: Post-abortion Syndrome

According to pro-life counselors, post-abortion syndrome is a real and serious condition. Post-abortion syndrome is said to be similar to post-traumatic stress disorder (PTSD), a psychological disorder suffered by war veterans and survivors of extreme abuse. Sufferers of both disorders have nightmares and flashbacks (repeated relivings of painful memories while awake). Both disorders may include outbursts of anger, alternating with periods of emotional numbness in which they find it difficult to care about anything. Their personal relationships and job performance suffer, and they often avoid people or places that remind them of the stressful event.

The National Right to Life Educational Trust Fund reports a long list of post-abortion syndrome

Post-abortion Syndrome Support Groups

Support groups exist for women who have post-abortion syndrome. The groups may meet in person or talk through online chat groups. Some of the groups are distinctly pro-choice or pro-life, while others are neutral. These groups are a safe place for women to share their feelings.

symptoms including guilt, depression, avoidance of children, and abuse of drugs or alcohol. In their view, women's relationships with men are expected to suffer after an abortion. Breakups and divorces are common, even if both people supported the abortion decision.

Women with post-abortion syndrome may suffer an overwhelming sense of anxiety, fear, or helplessness. Pro-life counselors report that more than 50 percent of women being treated for post-abortion syndrome have considered suicide—28 percent have actually attempted it.

The National Right to Life also claims that mothers who have aborted one or more pregnancies are more likely to abuse any children they do have.

PRO-CHOICE PERSPECTIVE: POST-ABORTION SYNDROME DOES NOT EXIST

The National Abortion Federation believes that post-abortion syndrome does not exist and has been invented as a strategy for advancing the pro-life agenda. The NAF claims that the feelings of sadness that women have after an abortion recede quickly. The primary emotions for post-abortive women, they say, are relief and happiness about returning

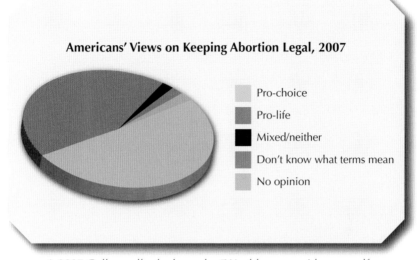

Americans' Views on Keeping Abortion Legal, 2007

- Pro-choice
- Pro-life
- Mixed/neither
- Don't know what terms mean
- No opinion

A 2007 Gallup poll asked people, "Would you consider yourself pro-choice or pro-life?" The results show, when pressed, most Americans say they are pro-choice.

to normal life. According to the NAF, the most stressful period of time for the woman is before the abortion, not after.

The American Psychological Association is a scientific organization that is neither pro-choice nor pro-life. In 1989, the association conducted a review of research on post-abortion psychological problems. They found no signs of post-abortion syndrome. The syndrome is not a scientifically recognized disorder.

Pro-life activists counter that the syndrome is quite real. They admit that much of the evidence is anecdotal, or based on personal stories rather than scientific data. But anecdotes are also compelling, they argue, and should not be discounted.

REGRET OVER ABORTIONS?

Do women feel regret years after having abortions? It depends on the woman. Both the pro-choice and pro-life advocates can find real people who tell true stories about how abortion affected them. Each side in the controversy selects the stories that best support their position. Some women see their abortions as overwhelmingly positive steps they took to take control of their lives. Others mourn their lost child and continue to regret their decision.

Psychologist Patricia Lunneborg has conducted more than 100 interviews with women who have had abortions and with abortion providers. Some of her results may be surprising. For example, most of the women she interviewed who had children prior to an abortion said their relationships with their children

Abortions and Breast Cancer

Many questionable reports are circulating that claim abortions increase a woman's risk of breast cancer. The National Cancer Institute gathered nearly 100 of the world's experts on the issue. The experts concluded that having an induced abortion or a natural miscarriage does not increase a woman's risk of breast cancer.

improved after the abortion. For many, it was a step toward setting limits, not only on the size of their families, but in their emotional lives as well. One of the women Lunneborg interviewed summed up her experience with abortion by saying, "Thank God I had the sense to do what I knew was right."[1]

Stories from women who regret their abortions are heartrending. Author Susan Neiburg Terkel reports that both women and men can have long-term emotional issues as a result of abortion. One man confessed that 20 years after his wife's abortion he "broke down and wept."[2]

Voices of the Abortion Debate

- Pro-life Voices

"I feel that the greatest destroyer of peace today is abortion, because it is a war against the child, a direct killing of the innocent child, murder by the mother herself."[3]

—*Mother Teresa,*
Winner of the Nobel Peace Prize in 1979

"Abortion is advocated only by persons who have themselves been born."[4]

—*Ronald Reagan, former U.S. President*

- Pro-choice Voices

"I have met thousands and thousands of pro-choice men and women. I have never met anyone who is pro-abortion."[5]

—*Hillary Clinton, U.S. Senator from*
New York and former First Lady

"I hope every woman in this country, whether they agree with *Roe* or they disagree with *Roe*, whether they themselves would make one decision or another, will come together and say: Pro-choice means that the government respects the individual, and isn't that really what our country is all about?"[6]

—*Barbara Boxer,*
U.S. Senator from California

One woman describes what she called "severe mental problems" involving flashbacks, self-hatred, and endless grieving years after her abortion.[7]

Is There a Right Answer?

Is abortion morally acceptable? The answer to this question must be decided by each individual. Should it be legal? This question is one of ongoing debate in a democracy. Abortion is never an easy decision, but not everyone needs to make that decision. Unplanned pregnancies can be avoided by abstaining from sex or by careful use of birth control. In this way, if a woman chooses to have children, it can be on her terms—quite apart from the abortion issue. ⌐

A teenage couple waits for the results of a store-bought pregnancy test.

TIMELINE

1821	1856	1873
Connecticut bans poison-induced abortions after the fourth month of pregnancy.	The American Medical Association lobbies to end legal abortion.	The Comstock Act makes it illegal to distribute information on birth control and abortion.

1960	1967	1973
Birth control pills are introduced.	Abortion becomes a felony.	*Roe v. Wade* Supreme Court ruling legalizes abortion.

1890	1916	1938
Abortion is prohibited in most states unless it is necessary to save the mother's life.	Margaret Sanger opens the first birth control clinic in the United States.	Doctors are allowed to give birth control information to their patients.

1976	1977	1981
The Supreme Court makes it illegal to force a married woman to obtain her husband's consent before having an abortion.	Law rules that Medicaid will not pay for abortions, except in cases of rape, incest, or when a mother's health is at risk.	Medicaid does not pay for any abortions, even when a mother's health is at risk.

TIMELINE

1981	1989	1990
Supreme Court rules that pregnant minors can petition the court for abortion without parental notification.	The Supreme Court overturns a Missouri state law stating that life begins at conception and banning use of public facilities for abortion.	The Supreme Court rules that states may require a minor to obtain parental consent before having an abortion.

1994	1995–1996	2003
The Freedom of Access to Clinic Entrances (FACE) Act is passed in May.	The abortion debate focuses on state bans of partial-birth abortions.	President George W. Bush signs a bill banning partial-birth abortion.

1992

In *Planned Parenthood v. Casey*, the Supreme Court reaffirms *Roe* but allows a mandatory 24-hour waiting period before abortion.

1993

Medicaid again pays for abortions in cases of rape, incest, or where a risk is posed to the mother's health.

1994

In February, the Supreme Court declares that protestors who block access to clinics can be prosecuted in *NOW v. Scheidler.*

2006

The FDA approves nonprescription sales of Plan B for women 18 and older.

2007

The Supreme Court upholds a law banning partial-birth abortion.

ESSENTIAL FACTS

AT ISSUE

Pro-life position

❖ Life begins at conception. All unborn children, from fertilized ova through delivery, should be endowed with full human rights.

❖ Both medical and surgical abortions are dangerous for the woman and usually leave her with permanent physical, psychological, and emotional scarring.

❖ The fetus feels extreme pain during an abortion.

❖ *Roe v. Wade* should be overturned and abortion made illegal.

Pro-choice position

❖ Legal abortions are safe abortions. If abortion is made illegal, abortions will not stop. They will return to unsanitary clinics and be performed by unqualified providers. The result will be more women dying of botched abortions.

❖ The risks of medical and surgical abortion are low. The risk of abortion is less than the risk of taking a pregnancy to term. Most women recover quickly from the stress of an abortion.

❖ The fetus cannot feel pain until the twenty-ninth week of development. At this point, abortions are banned except to preserve the life or health of the mother.

❖ *Roe v. Wade* is essential to women's equality and ability to control their own destiny. It must be preserved.

"Morally pro-life but legally pro-choice" position

❖ Abortion is not murder. However, the fetus deserves special respect, and abortion is morally wrong.

❖ It is also morally wrong to force a woman to nurture a baby in her uterus, perhaps at the cost of her own well-being.

❖ Abortion should be discouraged while it remains legal.

Key Groups on the Abortion Debate

Pro-life:

❖ National Right to Life Committee (NRLC)

❖ Birthright International

Pro-choice:

❖ Planned Parenthood Federation of America

❖ National Abortion Rights Action League (NARAL)

❖ National Organization for Women (NOW)

Key Dates

1890 Abortion becomes illegal in most states.

1967 Abortion becomes a U.S. felony.

1973 *Roe v. Wade* ruling by the Supreme Court makes abortion legal.

2003 U.S. law bans partial-birth abortion.

Quotes

"I feel that the greatest destroyer of peace today is abortion, because it is a war against the child, a direct killing of the innocent child, murder by the mother herself." —*Mother Teresa*

"I hope every woman in this country, whether they agree with *Roe* or they disagree with *Roe*, whether they themselves would make one decision or another, will come together and say: Pro-choice means that the government respects the individual, and isn't that really what our country is all about?" —*Barbara Boxer*

ADDITIONAL RESOURCES

SELECT BIBLIOGRAPHY

Lunneborg, Patricia. *Abortion: A Positive Decision*. New York: Bergin and Garvey, 1992.

National Right to Life. <http://www.nrlc.org>.

Olasky, Marvin. *Abortion Rites: A Social History of Abortion in America*. Washington, D.C: Regnery Publishing, Inc., 1995.

"Overview of Abortion: An Unsolvable Dilemma?" <http://www.religioustolerance.org/abo_over.htm>.

Sloan, Don and Paula Hartz. *Abortion: A Doctor's Perspective, a Woman's Dilemma*. New York: Donald I. Fine, Inc., 1992.

FURTHER READING

Almond, Lucinda, ed. *The Abortion Controversy*. Detroit, MI: Greenhaven Press, 2007.

Marcovitz, Hal. *Abortion*. Broomall, PA: Mason Crest Publishers, 2007.

Torr, James, ed. *Abortion: Opposing Viewpoints*. Farmington Hills, MI: Greenhaven, 2006.

WEB LINKS

To learn more about abortion, visit ABDO Publishing Company on the World Wide Web at **www.abdopublishing.com**. Web sites about abortion are featured on our Book Links page. These links are routinely monitored and updated to provide the most current information available.

FOR MORE INFORMATION

National Abortion Rights Action League (NARAL)
1156 15th Street, NW, Suite 700, Washington, DC 20005
202-973-3000
www.naral.org
NARAL is a pro-choice grassroots organization with more than one million members. It lobbies on the state and national level to influence laws regarding women's reproductive rights.

National Right to Life Committee (NRLC)
512 10th Street NW, Washington, DC 20004
202-626-8800
www.nrlc.org
This national pro-life organization includes 3,000 chapters throughout the United States. The NRLC is a lobbying group as well as a clearinghouse of information for pro-life activists.

GLOSSARY

abstinence

Not having sex.

anesthesia

Using drugs to make a patient insensitive to pain before surgery.

child support

Regular payments of money from the noncustodial parent (who does not live with the child) to the custodial parent to cover some or all of the expenses of a child.

class-action lawsuit

A lawsuit brought on behalf of a large group of people, most of whom are not involved in the trial proceedings.

conception

The beginning of a pregnancy when a sperm from the man fertilizes an ova, or egg cell, from the woman.

consent

Permission.

contraception

Birth control.

embryo

The term for an unborn child up to eight weeks of gestation.

fetus

The term for an unborn baby after eight weeks of development.

harassment

Behavior, often repeated, that causes stress, worry, alarm, or annoyance to another person.

implanting

When a fertilized egg attaches securely into the wall of the uterus.

incest

> The crime of an adult having sexual relations with someone closely related to him or her.

minor

> A young person who has not yet reached the age of legal adulthood.

partial-birth abortion

> A form of late-term abortion, now banned in the United States, in which the fetus is partially removed from the womb before it is aborted.

paternity

> The determination of who the father of a child is.

post-abortive

> After an abortion.

premature

> The term for a baby born before it has completed the third trimester of development; one born before 37 weeks.

prenatal

> Before birth.

sterile

> Unable to have children.

term

> End; "taking a pregnancy to term" refers to letting the fetus develop until it is ready to be born.

trimester

> A third of the total time of a pregnancy.

ultrasound

> A technique for getting an image of the inside of the body, or of a fetus, by using high-energy sound waves.

SOURCE NOTES

Chapter 1. A Sensitive Subject

None.

Chapter 2. Abortions from Past to Present

1. Marvin Olasky. *Abortion Rites: A Social History of Abortion in America.* Washington, D.C.: Regnary Publishing, Inc., 1995.

Chapter 3. Our Changing Society

None.

Chapter 4. Controversy and Democracy

1. Dirk Johnson. "Jury Rules That Anti-Abortion Leaders Violated Racketeering Laws." *The New York Times.* 21 Apr. 1998.

2. David John Marley. "How the Christian Right Borrowed the Rhetoric of the Civil Rights Movement." *History News Network.* 31 May 2004. 6 Sept. 2007 <http://hnn.us/articles/5398.html>.

3. R.A. Terry. "Operation Rescue." *Montana Human Rights Network.* 1988. 5 Sept. 2007 <http://www.mhrn.org/publications/fact%20 sheets%20and%20adivsories/OperationRescue.pdf>.

4. Ibid.

Chapter 5. The Gray Zone

1. "Abortion: The Hard Cases." *Michigan Right to Life*. 20 Aug. 2007 <http://www.rtl.org/html/Abortion/abortion_hard_cases.html>.

2. "Defending the Pro-Life View." Canadian Centre for Bio-Ethical Reform. 20 Aug. 2007 <http://www.ccbrinfo.ca/faq.html>.

3. Ann Harmon. "The Problem with an Almost-Perfect Genetic World." *The New York Times*. 20 Nov. 2005.

Chapter 6. Shifting Boundaries

None.

Chapter 7. Abortion on the International Scene

None.

Chapter 8. Abortion and Families

1. "Ex-Boyfriend Can't Stop Abortion." CBS News. 5 Aug. 2002. 20 Aug. 2007 <http://www.cbsnews.com/stories/2002/07/25/politics/main516284.shtml>.

Chapter 9. Psychological Effects of Abortion

1. Patricia Lunneborg. *Abortion: A Positive Decision*. New York: Bergin and Garvey, 1992.

2. Susan Neiburg Terkel. *Abortion: Facing the Issues*. New York: Franklin Watts, 1988.

3. Mother Teresa of Calcutta. "Whatever You Did unto One of the Least, You Did unto Me." The Augustine Club at Columbia University. 3 Feb. 1994. 20 Aug. 2007 <http://www.columbia.edu/cu/augustine/arch/teresa94.html>.

4. Ronald Reagan. "Abortion." FamousQuotes.com. 20 Aug. 2007 <http://www.famousquotes.com/search.php?cat=1&search=Abortion>.

5. Tom Head. "Top 10 Pro-Choice Quotes." About.com: Civil Liberties. 20 Aug. 2007 <http://civilliberty.about.com/od/abortion/tp/choice_quotes.htm>.

6. "Barbara Boxer Quotes." Brainy Quote. 20 Aug. 2007 <http://www.brainyquote.com/quotes/authors/b/barbara_boxer.html>.

7. Susan Neiburg Terkel. *Abortion: Facing the Issues*. New York: Franklin Watts, 1988.

INDEX

ABOUT THE AUTHOR

Courtney Farrell taught biology and microbiology for ten years at Front Range Community College in Colorado, but is now a full-time science writer. She creates encyclopedia articles, materials for college-level biology textbooks, and occasional magazine articles on ranching or parenting. She holds a master's degree in zoology and is interested in conservation and sustainability issues. Farrell is certified as a designer and teacher of Permaculture, a type of organic agriculture. She lives with her husband and sons on a ranch in the mountains of Colorado.

PHOTO CREDITS